PUBLIC
LIBRARY
ASSOCIATION
A division of the American Library Association

P9-DBN-552

THE GUIDE TO BASIC RESUME WRITING

Job and Career Information Services
Committee of the Adult
Lifelong Learning Section

Public Library Association
American Library Association

VGM Career Horizons
a division of *NTC Publishing Group*
Lincolnwood, Illinois USA

Library of Congress Cataloging-in-Publication Data

The Guide to basic resume writing / Job and Career Information
  Services Committee of the Adult Lifelong Learning Section, Public
  Library Association [and] American Library Association.

     p.   cm.
  ISBN 0-8442-8123-9 (softbound) : $7.95
1. Résumés (Employment)—Handbooks, manuals, etc. I. Public
Library Association. Job and Career Information Services Committee.
II. American Library Association.
HF5383.G727 1991
650.14—dc20   90-50722
                                                    CIP

1993 Printing

Published by VGM Career Horizons, a division of NTC Publishing Group.
4255 West Touhy Avenue, Lincolnwood (Chicago), Illinois 60646-1975 U.S.A.

 2 3 4 5 6 7 8 9 VP 9 8 7 6 5 4

Contents

Purpose

The Job and Career Information Services Committee was formed by and for public librarians whose public includes job seekers. All members of the committee work with job and career information to some degree. They wrote this book to fill a need expressed by their patrons and many other librarians.

Knowing that the book's usefulness extends beyond library use, the committee submitted it to VGM Career Horizons. Their acceptance assures the broad distribution the committee desired.

Marianne C. Fairfield
President-Elect
Adult Lifelong Learning Section
Public Library Association
American Library Association

Acknowledgments

The Job and Career Information Services Committee of the Adult Lifelong Learning Section of the Public Library Division of the American Library Association prepared *The Guide to Basic Resume Writing*. Members of the committee who contributed materials are:

Marianne Fairfield	Cuyahoga County (Ohio) Public Library
Barbara Fellows	Public Library of Columbus and Franklin County (Ohio)
Vera A. Green	Carnegie Library of Pittsburgh
Steven P. Lane	Army Technical Information Center, Ft. Lewis, Washington
Jeanne Patterson	Cuyahoga County (Ohio) Public Library
Erlinda Regner	Chicago Public Library
Mary Jo Ryan	Nebraska Library Commission
Ricky Fairtile-Wasserman	Queensborough (New York) Public Library

Special thanks go to Marianne Fairfield and Jeanne Patterson for editing the manuscript; to Virginia Fore, Enoch Pratt, Free Library (Baltimore), and Jane Heiser, State Library of California, for checking the vocabulary; to Laura Fliger and Brenda Corder, student interns from the University of Nebraska for contributing resumes; to Nancy Fisher, Wickliffe (Ohio) Public Library, John Lonsak, and Hedy Werner, Cuyahoga County Public Library, for final preparation and proofreading; and to Nancy Henry, Cuyahoga County Public Library, for typing the manuscript.

We also acknowledge and thank all the public and academic libraries that submitted sample resumes.

Foreword

In promoting the expansion of the public library movement in the United States, one of the chief goals behind Andrew Carnegie's widespread philanthropy was the creation of an uniquely American institution that would someday evolve into the "people's university." Through the years, the American public library has clung fast to this goal, offering an array of informational services and lifelong learning opportunities for individuals from infancy through advanced old age that serve to support and enhance a variety of human undertakings.

When initially focusing on the contemporary public library, many may fail to fully realize the tremendous career-related offerings available within almost any public library setting: occupational guides, business/organizational reports, resume preparation materials, and perhaps the most essential resource of all—trained and experienced librarians to aid library users in better identifying and utilizing the informational tools needed in their job-seeking pursuits. Now, under the auspices of the Job and Career Information Services Committee of the Public Library Association (a division of the American Library Association), librarians, who are the ultimate information providers, have compiled a resume-writing guide that is our profession's consummate response to its commitment to assist with lifelong learning activities—including career enhancement.

Whether you are considering a job or career change, reentering the job market following a long- or short-term absence, or seeking your first job, this thoughtful, complete, and easy-to-use resume guide is the perfect aid for you. Developed by librarians with years of experience in collecting and providing job assistance information, *The Guide to Basic Resume Writing* is one of the best resources available for those seeking employment in today's demanding and highly competitive job market.

Charles M. Brown
President
Public Library Association

Introduction

In today's job market, it is very important to have all of your facts organized before you start your job search. Resumes are helpful to everyone, not only professionals. This guide has been designed to fill the gap identified by many librarians and professional job counselors who need basic guidelines for resume writing and sample resumes to meet the needs of low skilled clients. With help from an instructor, this book can be used by adults enrolled in basic education or workplace literacy classes. More skilled adults can use it independently. The guide also contains a selected bibliography of other resume-writing books that are useful for those with higher skills.

PART I

General Guidelines for Writing Resumes

Why You Need a Resume

A resume is a short advertisement of your skills in outline form. It is a tool in which you present yourself to a would-be employer.

Your resume may be your only chance to tell an employer about the skills, experience, and training that qualify you for a special job. It is important for you to take the time to write the best resume you can.

Your resume should contain all the facts that show you qualify for a job. The items you choose to highlight should closely match the requirements stated in the job description.

What the Employer Needs to Know

Who you are	Name, address, telephone number
What job you want	Objective Statement: A phrase or brief paragraph stating what you want to do. You can use a job title.
What you have done	Qualifications: A summary of your strengths, paid and unpaid experience, accomplishments, and education
What you can do	Your skills

Before You Write Your Resume

Think about all your past jobs, activities, and education:

- what you have learned
- responsibilities you have assumed
- what you have accomplished
- how you have contributed
- why you have been effective

- all of your abilities and skills
- when you went to school
- special training

Highlighting your skills and accomplishments may seem like bragging, but it is appropriate and even necessary to do so in a resume. Your resume tells the employer about you and the value you place on your skills. Because we are not used to judging ourselves in this way, we sometimes sell ourselves short by downplaying or failing to mention important skills.

A good way to start is to make a list of everything:

1. *Work History.* Include paid and volunteer work. Listing the volunteer work is very important, especially if you are a student or a person returning to paid employment. List the names of employers, the dates you worked at each job, and what you did. Make sure you have correct spelling for all names.

2. *Education and Training.* Start with high school. Include the names of the schools; the dates you attended each; your major course of study (or major courses); and the degrees, diplomas, and certificates you earned. Include all continuing education, adult education, and on-the-job training you have had. List honors, internships, and scholarships awarded if they are relevant.

3. *Special Work-related Skills.* Include skills such as the ability to operate a computer or word processor, ability to operate special machinery or equipment, and ability to supervise another worker or work crew.

4. *Accomplishments and Special Projects.* For example: helping increase sales or income during any of your jobs; working full time or managing a home while taking courses to complete your diploma or degree; or completing a difficult building project.

Writing Your Resume

If you are applying for more than one job, you may need more than one resume. You will have to highlight different skills for different jobs.

What to and What not to Write

- Include career or job objective.

- Include all work experience and education.

- Include any strengths and other positive information.

- Do not include reasons why you left any job.

- Do not list salaries for any job.

- Do not include information on date of birth, marital status, religion, ethnic group, height, weight, or health.

- Do not include names of supervisors or references. You may end your resume with the statement: "References available on request," but this is optional.

- Do not use the word *Resume* on the top of the page.

What a Resume Should Look Like

Your resume should be eye-catching and easy to read. Above all, it should look professional. Many professional secretarial and printing services cost less than you might expect. They are familiar with preparing resumes, and they know how to make a resume look good. If you prepare your resume on your own, keep the following tips in mind:

- Make a point to highlight the points you want the reader to notice.

- Short phrases are easier to read than long sentences and paragraphs.

- Use an outline format and leave lots of white space—wide margins and space between sections.

- Use dashes --- or dots . . . or asterisks ***, different kinds of type, and underlining to guide the eye.

- Line up major headings to make the resume easy to scan.

- Find a way to have your resume typed perfectly on a high quality electric typewriter or word processor.

- Have at least three other people proofread your resume to make sure all spelling, grammar, punctuation, and information are correct.

- Choose good quality bond paper for your resume. White, ivory, or gray looks best.

- Make sure photocopies of your resume are of high quality.

Note: Many professionals consider one page to be the ideal length for a resume. This is a good rule to follow. It is better, however, to use two pages if necessary than to crowd so much on one page that it is hard to read.

Resume Formats

There is no single standard resume format. The format you choose can make a difference in the impression you make. It is important to choose a design and approach that is concise and effective. Ask yourself these questions:

- What in my background best proves I can do the job?
- Should I put my emphasis on my skills, or where I've worked, or on the courses that I've taken in school?
- What are my major selling points?

There are two basic types of resumes, chronological and functional. A *chronological resume* highlights your work history by date. A *functional resume* highlights your skills. From these two formats, a number of variations can be developed. The most common variations are combination resumes, targeted resumes, qualification briefs and marketing letters:

- The *combination resume* combines a section that highlights skills and a section on work history containing your job title, place of work, dates, responsibilities, and accomplishments.
- The *targeted resume* focuses on those skills and achievements that relate directly to a very specific job.
- The *qualifications brief* highlights the qualities, accomplishments, and abilities that show you are qualified for a particular job.
- The *marketing letter* presents resume information in letter form and may include work history or skills or both.

Chronological Format

The body of a chronological resume includes a listing of your work history, beginning with your most current job. Other sections may include a job objective; information on your education; a summary of skills, volunteer experiences, unions, and other word-related associations; and community activities.

- Information near the top of the page gets read most carefully. It is effective to state your job objective, then summarize your qualifications in a sentence or two before presenting your work history.
- The section on work history may be titled *Work History, Job History, Employment, or Experience.* List your latest employment first, then previous jobs according to dates. State your job title, employer, and dates of employment

for each job. You may include addresses, but use city and state only.

Under each job title explain exactly what your duties and responsibilities were, what skills you learned, and what you achieved. It is important to use words that tell how much, how often, how well, and what results were produced.

- List your formal education and training in a section titled *Education, Training,* or both. The most recent schooling should be listed first. This section may be presented either before or after your work history. It will depend on which is most important in the qualifications the employer is looking for.

A chronological format is useful when:

- the amount of time on each job (paid or unpaid) may be viewed as a strength

- your work experience prepares you for your job objective

- former job titles or employers are impressive

- you want to show your advancement in a company or a field of work

Functional Format

The body of a functional resume highlights your major skill areas. Emphasis is placed on your skills, not on work experience. Job titles, dates or names of employers should be left out. However, other sections may include a job objective, information on education, a summary of abilities, unions, and other work-related associations.

You may label the section describing your skills in a variety of ways, such as:

- Skills

- Abilities

- Accomplishments

- Experience

- Areas of competence

Cluster your skills gained through both paid and unpaid experiences under one heading. For example, if you typed on one job, did filing on another job, and acted as a receptionist someplace else, these activities could be listed under the heading of *Office Skills:*

- Typed correspondence and statistical reports for administrative staff of two small companies (60wpm).
- Established and maintained an effective filing system with over 350 regular customers (auto service center).
- Acted as receptionist in local bank and front office of auto service center.

Unpaid experience may be listed in the same way:

- Typed correspondence for church staff (60wpm).

Use descriptive statements to show your skills—statements that specify (how much?, how often?) and qualify (how well?, results achieved?). Include a section listing your formal education, putting your most recent first.
A functional resume is useful when:

- you want to change career fields and need to identify skills that may be used in a new situation.
- you are short on work experience but still have skills that can be identified and grouped.
- you want to enter or reenter paid employment and have acquired skills through unpaid or paid experience.
- you have had many different work experiences that are not directly related to the job you're seeking—for example: managing a pet shop, repairing appliances, serving as a teacher's aide.

Combination Resume

A combination resume uses parts of a functional and parts of a chronological resume. Follow the rules for writing the functional and the chronological resumes. The combination resume is useful when you have acquired a number of skills while progressing on one or several jobs.

Targeted Resume

The body of the targeted resume focuses on those abilities and duties from past jobs that are directly related to the specific job for which you are applying.

- Remember that information near the top of the page gets read most carefully. List first all the skills and work experience that are closely related to the advertised position.
- The targeted resume is useful when you have specific qualifications for a specific job. It *must* be prepared for one position only.

Qualifications Brief

The body of the qualifications brief highlights the qualities, accomplishments, and abilities that show you are suited (qualified) for a particular job.

Marketing Letter

The marketing letter presents resume information in letter form. It may include work history, skills, or both. It is more like a letter than a resume, and it is often used in place of both. See part III on cover letters for more details.

How to Get the Professional Look

How your resume looks is sometimes almost as important as what your resume says. Be sure to make your resume look as professional as possible by making it both appealing to the eye and easy to follow. Use the following pointers to help you get the professional look that you want.

A heading presents your name, address, and telephone number. Express your creativity in designing a heading. You may also wish to use it for cover letters, thank-you notes, and other correspondence. Be sure your name stands out. Here are some examples of headings:

JOHN JONES

222 Maple Street, Solon, Ohio 44139   216/555-9753

ELLEN RODRIGUEZ

826 Elm Street
Cleveland, Ohio 44106
216/555-8308

ELLEN RODRIGUEZ
826 Elm Street, Cleveland, Ohio 44106 (216) 555-8308

DWANDA JONES

222 Maple Street
Solon, Ohio 44139

216-555-4353

Job/Career Objective

It is usually helpful to state a job and/or career objective describing the focus of your job search. This objective statement:

- is a summary, or lead statement, for the rest of your resume
- focuses on what you can do
- states how you can be of help to the employer (it is not a statement of personal goals)
- identifies for the employer where and how you might fit in the organization
- tells the employer that you have definite goals

If you include a job objective, it is always the first item on your resume following your heading. The objective statement may be labeled "Objective," "Job Objective," "Job Target," "Career Objective," "Employment Objective," or "Professional Objective."

The statement may be one word, a job title, a phrase, a sentence fragment, or a sentence including the job title or career area. The simplest objective statement may be just the name of the position or job area. Keep the following tips in mind:

- Use a sentence that contains action verbs.
- Tell the employer what you intend to do, such as sell, supervise, clean, fix, build, or operate.
- Avoid general statements, such as "Seeking a responsible position in a progressive organization with opportunity for advancement." Such statements fail to tell the employer anything useful or specific about you or your desires.

The following are examples of job/career objective statements:

OBJECTIVE: A position managing a small medical office using my supervisory, organizational, and secretarial skills.

CAREER
OBJECTIVE: Transportation Coordinator or Supervisor,
                using management experience and communication skills.

OBJECTIVE
Industrial Sales

COMPUTER PROGRAMMER–SYSTEMS ANALYST

Qualifications Summary

This brief summary of your qualifications, background, and strengths will highlight information about you that you want an employer to know. Place the qualifications summary immediately following the job/career objective statement. Be sure to keep these things in mind:

- Determine what you most want an employer to know about you.
- List the ideas you want to get across.
- Ask yourself the reasons an employer should hire you.
- Translate your specific experiences into general abilities. These experiences may include length and type of work, personality characteristics, special areas of expertise, and education/training.

Here are some examples of qualifications summaries:

OBJECTIVE
A position in production using my background in computerized and non-computerized assembly

SUMMARY
Three years experience with computerized assembly line production ten years experience as a journeyman machinist

---

Quality Control/Manufacturing Technician
QUALIFICATIONS

- 1 year Quality Control Technician

- 8½ years Manufacturing Technician

- Worked with statistical quality control, material efficiency, labor efficiency, and random sampling

- Involved in research and development of new products in quartz semiconductor industry.

A position in management that will utilize my administrative and supervisory experience
EXPERIENCE IN:
. . . . Administration
. . . . Forecasting
. . . . Recruiting and Training
. . . . Credit Underwriting
. . . . Loan Organization
. . . . Secondary Market Operation

Body of the Resume

The body of the resume allows you to showcase your experience (paid and unpaid) and your skills. Writing this section was discussed earlier in Part I under the heading "Writing Your Resume." You may wish to reread this section.

Remember these important guidelines while writing the body of your resume:

- Start with the most important or most time-consuming task.

- Use action verbs to describe tasks.
- Be consistent in use of verb tense, at least in each section. For a current job, use the present tense (*type, organize*) or, say "Responsible for" (*typing, organizing*). Use past tense (*typed, organized*) for former experience.
- Think beyond your everyday responsibilities. List the things you feel good about having done and examples of recognition you have received.
- Choose concise, short, postcard-like phrases.
- Tell quantity information (how much? how many?) you did and how well you did it.
- When describing skills, choose a word or phrase to head each category. Similar activities, experiences, responsibilities, and tasks should be grouped together.

Education

The section on educational background should include all your formal training, workshops, seminars, and informal training that relate to the job for which you are applying. List apprenticeships and on-the-job training in this section, also.

You may place this section anywhere in the resume, depending on how important you think your education is. For example, if you've recently graduated from a program of study and haven't had any related work experience, you may place your educational achievements near the top of the resume. If you haven't been in school for a few years, you may want to place your education section after your work experience section, at the end of the resume.

No matter where you place the section on education, be sure to include:

- educational and training experiences (most recent first)
- workshops, seminars, and continuing education programs that relate to your objective
- apprenticeships and on-the-job training
- school-related activities, such as honors, offices held, and significant activities, if they are related to your objective
- the name of the institution, its location, your diploma or certification or degree, and dates of completion

If you attended college mention college courses taken, college major and minor, and any special requirements met, if they are related to your objective. Also mention any college or training expenses you earned on your own.

PART II

Sample Resumes

The sample resumes presented in this part are based on actual resumes prepared with the help of practicing librarians. Each has been used successfully by the type of job seeker described before each sample. No one resume will fit your situation exactly, but one or several studied together may give you the ideas you need to design your own resume. At the end of this part, there are several resumes in Spanish for Spanish speakers who are applying for jobs in a Spanish-speaking setting.

Woman Returning to Work

A woman reentering the work place after an extended period away from the job market must convince a prospective employer that she has skills that she acquired as a homemaker and participant in community affairs.

Women tend to belittle their jobs as full-time homemakers and see little relationship between the home and the paid workplace. Daily activities, such as time and money management, organization of schedules, teaching, nutrition, and many more jobs, are marketable skills. An unpaid job does not mean that the job does not require competence. It takes as much skill to work in a volunteer position as in a paid one.

Some counselors recommend an information (marketing) letter instead of a resume. It can be tailored to focus on specific skills. Gaps in employment won't show up as conspicuously. (See Part 3 for more information on the marketing letter.)

A functional resume will emphasize the skills used as homemaker or volunteer. Recent and important activities can be stressed, and employment gaps will not be as evident. Do not list personal information such as age, health, marital status, or number of children.

Decide what skills to include in your resume—usually those dealing with data, people, and things—then choose those you wish to emphasize. List the most important ones first, using language of the field to which you are applying. (Reading newspaper ads and trade publications can help you identify the proper language.) In listing your skills, there is no need to distinguish those used in unpaid from those used in paid experience.

Sample Resume
Woman Returning to Work

Joan Jackson
258 Old Farm Road
Dublin, Ohio 43217
614-555-0961

Management/Organization:
— Managed "Friends of the Library" Bookstore and Special Booksales, raising $7,500 annually
— Coordinated TWIGS Christmas Bazaar which made a profit of $15,000
— Served as President of School Parent/Teacher Association
— Organized Statewide Girl Scout Weekend Jamboree for 1,500 scouts

Teaching/Training:
— Tutored English as a Second Language student for four years
— Served as docent for Library tours for school children
— Acted as Room Mother to aid classroom teacher
— Conducted workshops for tutors for adult new readers
— Worked as Girl Scout Troop Leader for three years

Work History:

1975–Present	Volunteer with Public Library of Columbus and Franklin County, Columbus Literacy Council, Dublin Public Schools, Girl Scouts of America, TWIGS and other community associations
1972–1975	Caseworker, Franklin County Human Services Department — provided counseling for families needing public assistance
1969–1971	Library Assistant, Bexley Public Library — provided reader's advisory and reference help to library patrons

Education:

1969	BA Sociology, Ohio University
1985	Courses at Franklin University in Introduction to Microcomputers, Word Processing and File Management
References:	Furnished on request

15

Skilled Tradesperson

If you are a tradesperson, the employer is interested in what you can do. Your resume should tell an employer all the skills that you have. The types of machines that you can operate shows that you can learn to operate others. It is important that you tell about the special licenses that you have.

If the occupation has a union, it is important that you list the type and length of your apprenticeship. How long you have been a journeyman and what kinds of supervisory experience you have are also important. The types and length of schooling and a journeyman's card can help to get the job.

In the second of the following three resume examples, the employer can see that the welder has worked for the same company for seven years. This indicates to the employer that the applicant must have showed up for work and produced a good product. In your resume be sure to list the companies that you have worked for and approximately how long.

Remember, do not list personal information such as age, health, marital status, or number of children.

Sample Resume
Skilled Tradesperson

Sandra M. Smith
East 10118 11th Avenue
Spokane, WA 99225
(509) 555-1705

OBJECTIVE: Copier Repair Manager

EMPLOYMENT
HISTORY:
1975–Present   Saxon Copiers   Spokane, WA
               Copier Repair Technician. Responsible for servicing all makes of Saxon copiers.
               Prepared customer invoicing. Trained in laser copy technology.

1972–1975:   Kin Copier Service   Columbia, MO
               Evening Supervisor and Repair Technician. Supervised four employees in a copy
               service. Prepared accounting records and money deposits. Repaired IBM Series
               360 copy machines.

EDUCATION:
1971   Johnson County Junior College
               Overland Park, Kansas—A.A. in Electronics

REFERENCES: Available upon request

Sample Resume
Skilled Tradesperson

Greg Stevens
South 4807 Elm Street
Spokane, WA 99204

OCCUPATION: Certified Welder

SKILLS:
ARC, Gas, MIG, and TIG
Read Blueprints, Do Layouts
Repair generators, motors and plant equipment
Fabricate parts

Can also operate:

Forklift
Punch Press
Drill Press
Overhead Crane

COMPANIES
WORKED
FOR:
Crofoot's Welding and Fabrication, Mead, WA 1979 to present
Ideal Machine & Mfg. Inc., Tacoma WA 1975 to 1979
Popeye's Welding Company, Aurora, OR 1971 to 1975
Greenberry Tank & Iron, Corvallis, OR 1965 to 1971

REFERENCES: Wilber Hobson, East 908 Longfellow, Spokane, WA 99207
Chauncey Wakefield, North 2829 Mullan Road, Spokane, WA 99206
Robert Bartlett, East 13005 19th Street, Spokane, WA 99216

Sample Resume
Skilled Tradesperson

Bertha N. Norris
8602 Cadillac Drive
Pittsburgh, PA 15229

JOB OBJECTIVE: Administrative Secretary

CAPABILITIES   *WordPerfect 5.0
                    *dBase III Plus
                    *Lotus 1-2-3
                    *IBM PC
                    *NCR
                    *Tandy 1000
                    *Apple IIe
                    *Type 80/wpm

ACCOMPLISHMENTS   *Set up and managed client data base using dBase III Plus
                    *Kept records for office of fifteen using Lotus 1-2-3
                    *Devised back-up filing system and trained office staff to use it
                    *Kept time cards and salary records for office of fifteen
                    *Trained ten staff members in WordPerfect
                    *Made appointments and meeting arrangements for three administrators
                    *Made monthly travel bookings for administrator

EXPERIENCE   Office Manager/Secretary
                    PRDI, Pittsburgh, PA   7/88-Present

                    Dietary Aide (Temporary)
                    Allegheny Hospital, Pittsburgh, PA   3/88-5/88

                    Mail Sorter (Temporary)
                    ABC Mail Service, Pittsburgh, PA   1/88-2/88

                    Cashier
                    Church's Chicken, Pittsburgh, PA   1/87-12/87

EDUCATION   Bidwell Training Center, Pittsburgh, PA
                    Certificate, Word Processing   6/88

                    Connelley Skill Learning Center, Pittsburgh, PA
                    GED   6/79

Worker with Little Training or Skills

Many times, people forget that they have abilities that can get them better paying jobs. Even if they are not trained for a specific trade or profession, these abilities may be job related. Some of these abilities are:

- being able to speak other languages in addition to English
- having a valid driver's license
- getting along well with other people
- having experience working in groups with children or other adults
- supervising other people (children or adults)
- hobbies
- travel
- reading books and magazines about the kinds of work that you would like to do

The following resumes were written for people with some work experience but little training. These resumes include skills and other qualifications that were not actually performed on the job. If you lack the skills needed to work in a technical, trade, or professional job, you can still write a resume that will impress an employer. Your other abilities and skills are as important as formal training in some instances.

Sample Resume
Little Training/Skills

George West
1205 Orange Road
Nassau, NY 11736
(516) 555-0020

Job Objective: A position as a mechanic with a major automotive dealership

QUALIFICATIONS AND EXPERIENCE:
— Very strong interest in automobiles and trucks, and automotive equipment.
— Reading and studying Chilton's Automotive Industries, Car and Driver, Automotive
  Engineering, Home Mechanic.
— Attend automotive trade shows and auctions.
— Repair and rebuild cars and trucks.
— Completely rebuilt 1985 Chevrolet using old and new parts.
  I have been using this car regularly for the last five years.
— Advise others on mechanical problems and repair needs.
— Sold automotive parts and supplies.

EMPLOYMENT HISTORY:
1984–Present	Self-employed auto mechanic
1982–1984	John Grey's Automotive—Nassau, New York
1979–1982	Dale Mobile
1979–1981	Burger King
EDUCATION:	Nassau Community College—BOCES
	Equivalency Diploma
	Courses in—Automotive Technology
	Electronic Technology
1977–1979	Nassau Vocational High School
	Courses in—Automotive Repair
	Body Work
	Electronic Assembly

Sample Resume
Little Training/Skills

Leon Jackson
345 Wescott Place
Cincinnati, Ohio 44534

OBJECTIVE: To obtain a position as a stock clerk in a large retail organization

SKILLS: Manage flow of large stock volume
                           supervise inventory and prepare inventory reports
                        Operate warehouse carting and packing equipment
                        Accurate with figures
                        Reliable and dependable
                        Quick learner
                        Able to assume new responsibilities
                        Well-organized and efficient
                        Bilingual in Spanish and English

EMPLOYMENT HISTORY:
1984–PRESENT: Stockman, ACME supermarkets, main warehouse Livingston, Ohio
1981–1983:   Stockman, Laurel Drug Store
1979–1981:   Delivery Boy, Laurel Drug Store

EDUCATION:
1987:   High school equivalency diploma
1983–1985:   Cincinnati central vocational high school courses in building
                           maintenance and repair

Sample Resume
Little Training/Skills

Maria Delas
901 East Main Street
Flourville, PA 19701
(215) 555-3132

Job Objective: A position as a supervisor in a professional cleaning/domestic/housekeeping
service.

EXPERIENCE:
— Supervise others in cleaning residential/commercial offices.
— Clean private residences, commercial and professional offices.
— Employed as exclusive housekeeper.

EMPLOYMENT HISTORY:
1984–1986   Dial-a-Maid Industries
1983–1984   Exclusive Housekeeper for two private residences
1981–1983   Apex Cleaning Service
1980–1981   Self-employed house cleaner

OTHER QUALIFICATIONS:
• Speak, read, write fluent French, can speak Spanish
• Pennsylvania State Driver's License
• Can be bonded

EDUCATION:
1977–1980   Santa Rosa Secondary School—Barbados, West Indies

Sample Resume
Little Training/Skills

Lisa Barton
5500 Margarette Street
Apt. 10
Pittsburgh, PA 15220
412-555-1385

OBJECTIVE: Full-time, entry-level position as General Clerk

CAPABILITIES: *Knowledge of computerized operations
*Excellent filing skills
*Detail oriented
*Good organizational skills
*Excellent telephone technique
*Light typing experience
*Knowledge of ten-key adding machine
*Work well with customers and fellow employees

EXPERIENCE
12/89–6/90   Mail Delivery Clerk/Back-up Receptionist
Personnel Pool Temporary Agency: Pittsburgh, PA

Responsible for sorting and delivering office mail. Acted as receptionist as needed, answering phones, greeting visitors, filing.

10/89–4/90   Cashier
Foodland Super Market: Pittsburgh, PA

Responsible for running cash register, totaling receipts, bagging groceries.

8/89–12/89   Receptionist
Coastal Temporary Services: Pittsburgh, PA
Answered phones, made appointments for clients, greeted visitors, light typing.

6/87–10/88   General Clerk
VA Hospital: Pittsburgh, PA
Duties included typing forms, filing, answering phones.

EDUCATION
1988   Peabody High School: Pittsburgh, PA
Diploma

John Stout
5556 Wood Street
Pittsburgh, PA 15203
412-555-9944

JOB OBJECTIVE: Cashier

EDUCATION

Peabody High School, Pittsburgh, PA
Currently enrolled in GED class.

Conroy Education Center, Pittsburgh, PA
Training workshops for busboy, dishwasher, stockboy, and cashier.
9/89–6/90

EXPERIENCE

Dining Room Attendant
Wendy's, Pittsburgh, PA
4/90–Present

Duties include cleaning tables and floors, refilling condiment and paper goods containers, setting up salad bar.

Dishwasher
Wendy's, Pittsburgh, PA
1/90–4/90

Responsible for cleaning grills, cookers, cooking utensils and serving equipment. Met Department of Health Standards for Restaurants.

Stockboy
Super G Market, Pittsburgh, PA
1/89–1/90

Duties included stocking shelves, unpacking crates, and marking prices.

First-Time Job Seeker

The functional resume is the best type for first-time job seekers to use, since they probably have little work experience. The functional type allows first-time job seekers to stress their capabilities and accomplishments in school activities and in life.

The following resumes show how recent graduates present their qualifications for a job by concentrating on skills they have acquired rather than jobs they have held.

Sample Resume
First-Time Job Seeker (High School)

Karen Godfrey
1118 East 12th
Spokane, WA 99202
(509) 555-1700

JOB OBJECTIVE:

Responsible job using my secretarial skills and knowledge of office procedures.

EXPERIENCE:

Clerical Skills

Typed regular correspondence using a word processor. Operated photocopier, adding and postage machines as a temporary office worker for Kelly Temporary Services. Maintained alphabetical filing system, routed telephone calls and distributed mail.

As a volunteer secretary for Sacred Heart Hospital's Volunteer Coordinator, typed letters, answered telephones, maintained volunteer placement list and distributed placement materials.

Bookkeeping Skills

Typed invoices as a temporary office worker through Spokane Public School's, Project W.A.G.E.

As treasurer of a service club, processed account payables and provided quarterly financial reports.

EDUCATION:

Lewis and Clark High School, Spokane, WA. Diploma 1986.

REFERENCES:

Available on request.

Sample Resume
First-Time Job Seeker (High School)

Heather A. Smith
12434 Morningside Lane
Lincoln, NE 68504
(402) 555-0376

Objective:	Salesperson for retail clothing store.
Sales:	Sold magazines and novelty gifts as fundraising projects for Prom Committee.
	Sold advertising space to local businesses for school yearbook.
Customer Relations:	Greeted customers and seated them at local supper club. Handled cash register and assisted with inventory and purchasing work. Answered questions and took reservations by phone.
Organization/ Management:	Served as secretary of local Future Business Leaders of America chapter.
	Child care for two children ages 5 and 7. Planning activities for the children and preparing two healthy meals each day for them.
Work Experience: 1987–1988 (Summers)	Child care Mrs. Kathy Smith, Lincoln, NE
1989 (Summer)	Hostess/Cashier The Speakeasy Supper Club, Lincoln, NE
Education:	Lincoln Southeast High School—will graduate June 1991.
References:	Available upon request.

Linda J. Lane
10166 N.E. 112th Place
Kirkland, WA 99033
(206) 555-9622

JOB OBJECTIVE:	Management Trainee Position
EDUCATION:	Bachelor of Arts, Business Administration, Washington State University Pullman, Washington. 1987

  Concentration: Management
  Minor: Management Information Systems

MANAGEMENT:
- Managed sorority house kitchen
- Carried full course load
- Competed on swim team
- Served as sorority business manager
- Supervised kitchen ordering

ORGANIZATION:
- Organized and coordinated fund-raising events
- Billed members for sorority dues
- Inventoried kitchen supplies
- Scheduled thirty sorority members for kitchen duty
- Completed office tasks—filing, typing, and duplicating

COMMUNICATION:
- Motivated sorority members to meet organizational goals
- Prepared monthly financial statements
- Wrote column for campus newspaper

WORK
EXPERIENCE:

Business Manager, Alpha Delta Pi, Washington State University,
  Pullman, WA 1985–1987

REFERENCES: Confidential Placement File
Washington State University
Pullman, WA 99004

Sample Resume
First-Time Job Seeker (College)

MICHAEL TARSUS
798 NINTH STREET
OAKDALE, PA 15189
(412) 555-8495

OBJECTIVE:	Laboratory Assistant
EDUCATION:	B.S. Biology Westminster College, New Wilmington, PA June, 1990

ACCOMPLISHMENTS Histology Study
*Compared normal organ tissue of rats to tissue of rats given
 foreign substances
*Helped prepare specimens for SEM and TEM microscopes
*Observed specimens under microscopes and recorded
 observations
*Trained in Electron Microscopy

EXPERIENCE
1/89–6/90   Physical Therapy Aide
                 Harmerville Rehabilitation Center, Harmerville, PA

                 *Assisted patients with therapeutic exercise
                 *Researched spinal cord injury patients

2/88–5/88   Laboratory Proctor
                 Westminster College, New Wilmington, PA

                 *Prepared specimens and solutions for biology lab
                 *Designed lab tests
                 *Supervised lab and assignment reviews

ACTIVITIES   Sigma Alpha Fraternity
                 *Pledge Class President
                 *Pan-Hellenic Chairman
                 *Brother-of-the-Year 1990
                  Ambassadors Club
                 *Top salesman

Alisha M. Mitchell
3456 Thomas Avenue
Beatrice, NE 68506
(346) 555-3846

Employment Objective: To find a copywriting position with a small Midwestern advertising agency.

Communications:
— Prepared print and broadcast news releases for various clients.
— Assisted in organizing a joint public exposition and corresponding press day for several clients. Wrote letters to editors and businesspeople to tell them of the event. Assisted in preparing a schedule of events, coordinating site details, and finding speakers.
— Prepared a display for a client which was shown at the State Fair. Wrote display copy and handled layout of the display. Wrote and laid out an accompanying handout.

Sales:
— Sold ladies apparel. Assisted customers and answered questions about merchandise. Ran cash register and assisted with inventory work.

Work History:
  5/90–8/90   Communications Intern
              Kaplan Public Relations, Lincoln, NE
  8/89–5/90   Sales Associate
              Creative Designs, Beatrice, NE

Education:
— Will receive Associate of Applied Science degree in Communications from Southeast Community College (Beatrice campus) in May 1991.
  Emphasis: Business
  Courses: Radio/TV Advertising, News Writing and Reporting, Editing and Page Makeup, Publications Production, Photojournalism, and Management.
References: Available upon request.

Career Changer

Changing careers in today's work world is not unusual. Some people change jobs as many as eight times during their working lives and may also change careers as many as three times or more.

Some people change careers because they wind up in the wrong job or find dissatisfaction in their job. Others change because they are unable to keep up with new technology. Still others are forced into career changes because they have reached a dead end in their career or had to move to a location where there are no jobs available in their chosen career. You may find that your interests and needs have changed and, therefore, you too must change careers.

Whatever your reasons are for changing your career, there are some things you must think about when you choose your new career and begin to prepare your resume. First, you must evaluate your skills, abilities, education, and experience in relation to your new career choice. Can you match those elements with the minimum qualifications you will need in your new job? Second, are there enough jobs available so that you are not locked out of your new career? Next, you should learn what the outlook is for that career. Will there still be jobs available five or ten years from now? Are there opportunities for advancement, or will you hit another dead end after a few years in your new career?

Once you have given some thought to these things and are still determined to go ahead with your career change, you must prepare a resume that will market those skills and others that are transferable to your new career. You may have also acquired new skills through education and independent learning that directly relate to your new career choice. Such information is important to include in your resume. In these cases, the best resume format to use is the functional or skills-based resume. This format allows you to highlight your transferable skills, knowledge, and other related experience.

For example, you might be a librarian with many years of experience and you wish to go back into the field in which you were originally interested—political science. A realistic option for you might be to pursue a career as a professional political campaign or party manager. Much of the managerial, supervisory, and research experience gained as a librarian can certainly be utilized in the political arena. Further, your educational background and some of your early professional experience can be directly related to your new career choice. (See the following example for Catherine Kaye.)

Another example: A former typesetter is unable to find regular employment in the typesetting industry. So much of the work he used to do manually is now done by computers and computer operators instead of trained typesetters and compositors. However, his experience as a home owner and self-styled real estate expert led to completion of a real estate sales course and licensing exam. Now he is prepared to assume an entry-level sales position in the real estate industry. By doing his homework, this soon-to-be real estate tycoon learned that property is still the safest investment and that more and more people will be buying and selling property through the end of the century. By emphasizing his interests and recent training, this former typesetter should have no trouble finding a sales position. (See the sample resume for Douglas Adams.)

Sample Resume
Career Changer

Catherine Kaye
4301 Forest Park
Gardenia, California 92341

OBJECTIVE: Political campaign or party management

SUMMARY OF QUALIFICATIONS
— 15 years managerial and supervisory work in public service
— Project design and administration
— Staff recruitment, training and supervision
— Public and Media relations
— Sophisticated research skills
— Community Liaison
— Fund raising, grantmanship and fiscal management for budgets of several million dollars
— Expertise in political process and political action
— Campaign management for local union and school associations
— Excellent communication skills, both verbal and written
— Member/officer community action organization and local school associations

EMPLOYMENT HISTORY:

1980–PRESENT:	Managing Librarian Metropolitan Public Library, Gardenia, CA
1975–1980	Supervising Librarian, Hollywood Branch, Los Angeles County Public Library
1968–1975	Social Sciences Librarian, Westwood Branch, Los Angeles County Public Library
1965–1968	Political Science Fellow, American Federation of State, County and Municipal Employees
1964–1965	Librarian Intern, City of Los Angeles Municipal Library

EDUCATION

MA—	University of Southern California—1968 Political Science/Public Administration
MSLS—	University of California, Los Angeles—1965 Certified Public Librarian
BS—	Pepperdine University—Malibu—1963 Sociology/Political Science

OTHER INTERESTS
— International Politics and Government
— Reading
— Travel

REFERENCES MAY BE OBTAINED UPON REQUEST

Sample Resume
Career Changer

Douglas Adams
32 West 24 Street
New York, New York 10010

OBJECTIVE: Real estate sales position with a large agency

QUALIFICATIONS: — Licensed in real estate sales in New York State
                            — Certificate in real estate from La Guardia Community
                              College
                            — Twenty-five years experience as home owner and
                              landlord
                            — Applied knowledge of computer applications and
                              software

RELATED EXPERIENCE
                            — Trainee in real estate sales, ABCO Realty
                            — Researched, purchased and financed own home and
                              developed expertise in same
                            — Completed comprehensive course in real estate sales at
                              La Guardia Community College
                            — Marketed and sold retail products and developed good
                              customer relations for over twenty years
                            — Advised relatives and friends on real estate purchases

EMPLOYMENT HISTORY:
1984–Present   Proofreader, Jones and Walters, Inc.
                            Printing Services to the Financial Community
1972–1984:   Free-Lance Printer/Proofreader
1962–1972:   Oak Press
1955–1962:   Newark Typographers
1948–1955:   Delman Press Works, Inc.

EDUCATION:
— La Guardia Community College, Certificate in Real Estate
— Bramson Technical College, Computer Operations/Programming
     12 credits toward AAS degree
— City College of New York, Electrical Engineering
     6 credits

Sample Resume
Career Changer

Olivia Sanchez
2971 Roosevelt Street
Pittsburgh, PA 15205
(412) 555-6224

JOB OBJECTIVE   TRAVEL AGENT

EXPERIENCE
1989–1990   Reservationist
USAIR, Pittsburgh, PA

Made reservations and explained rates and routes to customers, using computerized system. Provided service at desk and over the telephone.

1987–1989   Reservationist
Avis Car Rentals, Los Angeles, CA

Responsible for making reservations, explaining rates and policies, completing and filing forms. Used computerized reservations system.

1984–1987   Caseworker Aide
Children and Youth Services of Allegheny County, Pittsburgh, PA

Assisted social workers in program to protect mentally and physically abused children and helped eliminate the abusive situation. Duties included assisting at interviews with children and parents, typing forms and reports, filing, answering telephones.

1982–1984   Clerk
Armed Forces Recruitment Office, Pittsburgh, PA

Prepared forms for military recruits.

EDUCATION
1981   Bradford Business School, Pittsburgh, PA
Certificate in Secretarial Science

1975   Connelly Skill Training Center for Adults
General Education Diploma

AWARDS   *Employee of the month at Avis

Dislocated Worker

A dislocated worker is a worker who has been laid off from his or her job because the company closed or moved away. These workers are often unable to find new jobs because there is no longer a need for their skills. A good example is workers in the steel industry. Many steel companies have closed because the United States now imports large amounts of steel. This is due to the fact that labor costs abroad make the price of foreign steel cheaper than the price of steel made here. Other industries are affected in the same way.

If you are a dislocated worker, you may have to get training to learn new job skills. You can get this training through a community (two-year) college, a government-funded job training program, or other reputable program. Your library has information about where you can get training.

Dislocated workers have to highlight skills that can be used in many different kinds of jobs. All of us have such skills. For example, if you worked in the steel industry, some of your skills might be useful in other manufacturing companies. If you know how to use special equipment or machinery or understand how to use different types of machines, you can probably operate machinery somewhere else. If you have enjoyed teaching others how to operate machinery, you can look for jobs that allow you to train others. If you think you have experience in other areas, whether or not it was paid experience, include such experience on your resume.

Also, ask yourself some questions.

1. Can I get a job in a different industry because I know about that industry?

2. Are some of the skills I have the same as the skills needed in the new industry?

3. Did I ever do volunteer work? What kinds? Are there any jobs I could get doing the same kind of work?

4. Is there a place I could move to where my industry still operates?

5. Is there something else I could do to make money, like starting my own small business?

6. Do I want to go to school to learn new job skills?

By answering these questions, you can learn more about yourself. This will make it easier for you to write a new resume. The following resume examples will also help you.

Sample Resume
Dislocated Worker

John W. Towne
Rural Route 1
Norfolk, Nebraska 68701
(401) 555-1234

AGRICULTURE
— Prepared soil, irrigation water, and plant tissue samples for laboratory analysis.
— Scheduled all purchasing and marketing.
— Implemented nutrition and waste management programs.
— Coordinated all agronomic operations.
— Supervised swine activities.

SUPERVISION AND MANAGEMENT
— Supervised 4 employees.
— Initiated all activities for a swine corporation.
— Managed record-keeping system.

SALES
— Expanded sales by 35% for area livestock nutrition dealers.
— Directed sales, distribution, and created new markets as a livestock nutrition dealer.
— Instructed and motivated dealers and employers.
— Scheduled producer meetings.

LIVESTOCK NUTRITION
— Collected water, complete feed and feedstuff samples for laboratory analysis.
— Analyzed nutritional needs of livestock.

EXTRA ACTIVITIES
— Managed budget and disbursements as church council treasurer for 6 years.
— Led and coordinated County Pork Producers as director and secretary for 3 years.
— Supervised and organized activities as Sunday school teacher for $3^{1/2}$ years—grade 3.

EDUCATION AND EXPERIENCE
1986–present Livestock Nutrition Dealer, Norfolk, NE.
1976–present Self-employed Agriculturalist, Norfolk, NE.
1973–1976 Swine Corporation Manager, De-Cla, Inc., Clatonia, NE.
1972–1973 Livestock Nutrition Salesperson, Ralston Purina Co., Omaha, NE.
1971 B.S. in Agriculture—University of Nebraska at Lincoln

REFERENCES AVAILABLE UPON REQUEST

Sample Resume
Dislocated Worker

Michael Murphy, Jr.
Rural Route 2
Athens, IA 51601
(515) 555-3276

Employment Objective

Veterinary Technical or any position where my experience in animal care can be used or expanded.

Experience

1980–Present **On-Call Veterinary Assistant,** Georgia County Veterinary Hospital, Nelson, IA.
*Assisted local veterinarian with minor medical emergencies
*Advised area farmers on the proper care and management of their livestock.
*Diagnosed livestock and pet diseases
*Instructed local farmers on proper disease prevention and treatment methods
*Delivered newborn calves, hogs, swine, and sheep
*Collected water, complete feed and feedstuff samples for laboratory analysis
*Conducted nutrition and vitamin experiments on area livestock

1972–Present **Self-employed Dairy Farmer,** Athens, IA.
*Initiated all administration activities of a dairy farm
*Hired, trained, and supervised 3 employees
*Managed financial record-keeping system
*Analyzed livestock nutritional needs
*Prepared and administered inoculations to control the outbreak and spread of disease
*Managed selection and breeding of dairy cattle through genetic engineering
*Delivered and bottle-nursed newborn calves

Education and Special Training

May 1988 Seminar on Livestock Nutrition. Pioneer Seed Company, Des Moines, IA.
June 1985 Mini-course on Veterinary Medicine. Health-Tech Medical Supplies, Inc., Omaha, NE.
1972 Bachelor of Agriculture, Iowa State University.

Extra Activities

Elected Vice-President, National Dairy Association
Organized Livestock Committee for the Sidney, Iowa Rodeo
Member, Georgia County, Iowa Agriculture Board
Member, Georgia County School Board

Sample Resume
Dislocated Worker (Blue-Collar Worker)

Mark Beiber
1937 Carnegie Drive
Calson City, Pennsylvania
(612) 555-9043

Employment Objective
A position where my skills and expertise in machine maintenance, assembly operations and
  shipping/receiving will be significant assets.

Employment History
March, 1976, to September, 1987, Kaplan Automotive, Nilyania, Ohio

Assembly Operator
— Maintained automotive production equipment on a weekly basis following complex
  maintenance procedures.
— Used precision measuring equipment on automobile door frames to assure consistent quality
  production.
— Assembled door frames accurately and consistently.

January, 1972 to February, 1976, Steadrite Distributors, Grand Isle, Ohio

Shipping Clerk
— Accurately processed paperwork and maintained records of over 100 industrial supply orders
  per week.
— Devised and refined a complex system of financial and inventory control to ensure effective
  and profitable warehouse operations
— Led a Labor-Management working team implementing a "just in time" delivery system.
— Instructed six shipping department assistants in the operation of the delivery system.

Education and Specialized Training
— Chief Clerical Assistant School, Fort Ives, Kentucky, June 1969 to September, 1970—Army filing
  systems, inventory control and office management.
— Nilyania High School, Nilyania, Ohio—Graduated June, 1968

Honors and Awards
"Employee of the month"—Kaplan Automotive, September, 1984.
Recognition for team leadership in exceeding door frame production quota for six consecutive months.

1971 Ft. Ives. Certificate of Initiative awarded by base commander to the enlisted man whose efforts
  "significantly improved soldier morale."

References Available upon Request

Older Worker

Age should not be considered a major difficulty for those over forty who are seeking work. In firms with more than 20 employees, workers are protected by the age discrimination law. Older employees with more and broader experience and a greater understanding of the world of work also have an extra edge over younger workers.

In preparing a resume, the older job hunter should emphasize maturity, skills, and experience. Although it is illegal to ask questions about age, a resume without any dates suggests that there may be something to hide and may create the impression that the job seeker is older than he or she really is.

All appropriate dates should be given. Do not give age or birth date or year of graduation. Omit publication dates, if articles were written several years ago. In short, omit any clues that will screen you out.

Do not list all positions held. Group early work history by type of positions held. Omit unrelated jobs and those held for short periods. Be careful not to leave any time gaps. The resume does not need to be an all-inclusive document. It should not make you look out of date, but it should concentrate on present skills and activities. Only the most recent jobs that will convince an employer of your desirability need be listed. This type of resume should present specific qualifications for the job for which you are applying.

Many counselors suggest a functional resume because it highlights strengths and talents to the best advantage. Whatever format is selected, it should follow the standard directions for good resume writing. It should stress qualifications and experience. It should state the facts truthfully. Above all, it should be positive and present you as an achiever.

Sample Resume
Older Worker

John J. Johnson
738 Highland Avenue
Needham, Mass. 02194
417-555-7468

OBJECTIVE: Insurance Sales Manager

MANAGEMENT: Coordinated office operations in six-person agency. Trained clerical staff in processing claims. Developed sales campaign for introduction of new pension plan product. Recruited and trained sales staff.

SALES: Sold over $5 million in group insurance annually for the last three years. Led agency in monthly volume of sales three times in past year. Analyzed and presented proposals to 100 firms in past 12 months. Contributed to agency which won 1985 Agency of Year award for sales.

WORK EXPERIENCE:
1980–Present   Assistant Manager, Smithers Insurance Agency
1975–1980   Insurance Agent, John Hancock Insurance
Prior to 1975   Held positions in retail sales of appliances and home furnishings

EDUCATION: Northeastern University, BS Business Administration Coursework for CLU

PROFESSIONAL ORGANIZATIONS:
National Association of Life Underwriters
Boston Area Marketing Association

REFERENCES AVAILABLE ON REQUEST

Sample Resume
Older Worker

Mary L. Henderson
798 East Haven Road
West Hartford, Connecticut 06041
203/555-0921

OBJECTIVE:	Office Manager or Executive Secretary
WORK EXPERIENCE:	
1983–Present	Office manager—Jones and Matthews, Dentists, Inc. Duties include scheduling, bookkeeping, ordering supplies, billing, receptionist and scheduling functions.
1978–1983	Receptionist—Dailey, Hoyt, Parsons and Johnson, Attorneys. Duties included switchboard operation, typing and client contact.
Prior to 1978	Clerk-Typist—Simmons Temporary Agency. Held part-time temporary positions during the period when the family responsibilities prevented me from holding a full-time position.
SKILLS:	Knowledge of all office procedures and equipment. Typing: 90 words a minute Word Processing and PC Software use: Multimate and Lotus 1-2-3 Microcomputer familiarity: IBM-PC and Apple IIe
EDUCATION:	Hartford Business College, Secretarial Course, West Hartford Public Schools, Adult Education course in word processing and computer applications
VOLUNTEER ACTIVITIES:	
	West Hartford Schools: PTA Secretary, Fund-Raising Committee, Room Mother Easter Seals: Neighborhood Coordinator Cub Scouts: Den Mother

REFERENCES AVAILABLE UPON REQUEST

Worker Moving into Management

Climbing the career ladder can be very difficult. Employers want their supervisors and managers to have the experience they need to do the job. If you want to move up the ladder into a management position, you have to write a resume that convinces an employer that you can do the job. It is very important to use action words (see appendix C) to describe the skills you have. Many times you may also have to use numbers to impress an employer.

Ask yourself the following questions, taking into consideration both your paid and your volunteer work experience:

1. Have I ever supervised other people in a work situation?
2. Was I responsible for handling or managing a budget?
3. Did I ever create a new procedure to use in my job or for my company?
4. Did I ever organize activities, meetings, meals, or conferences for my company or organization?
5. Have I had any courses or other training that relates to the new position I want?
6. Have I been promoted at my company or have each of the jobs that I've had been better than the last?

Were you able to answer "Yes" to these questions? Do you have the facts to back up your answers? If so, then you are probably ready to look for jobs that include supervision and management. Your resume should say that you have the skills you need even if your job titles do not. Make sure you emphasize your knowledge and ability to move into a higher position. You must also say in your cover letter that you are ready to move up and accept the challenges and responsibilities of management.

Sample Resume
Worker Moving into Management

Jessica Lewin
7563 Oak Ridge
Havenwood, OH 44123
(614) 555-0005

Objective: A position as Director of a large Human Resources Department

QUALIFICATIONS:
— Screens and interviews support personnel in organization employing 1,500 full-time staff.
— Prepares evaluation reports.
— Conducts in-house training programs for support staff (average, 10 yearly).
— Recommends review of department procedures.
— Reviews and modifies organizational staff policies to comply with federal, state, and local regulations.
— Attends collective bargaining meetings.
— Attends grievance and other personnel-related hearings.
— Assists in recruitment activities on and off site.
— Assists in preparation of department budget.
— Supervised full-time staff of three.

EMPLOYMENT:
1984–Present   Drexel Corporation—Department of Human Resources, Department Assistant

1981–1984   Stevens College—Office of Personnel, Administrative Assistant

1979–1981   Stevens College—Office of Student Personnel, Recruiter

EDUCATION:
1982–1984   Ohio University—M.S. Human Resource Administration

1980–1982   Ohio University—M.S. Counseling and Industrial Relations

1976–1980   Stevens College—B.S. Major, Student Personnel, Minor, Sociology

Sample Resume
Worker Moving into Management

Jeanne Linne
4133 52 Avenue
Meadowmere, NY 11102

OBJECTIVE: Director of Fine and Applied Arts Department

SUMMARY OF QUALIFICATIONS:
— Over 40 years professional experience in fine and applied arts including fashion, painting, sculpture and ceramics, crafts, decoration and original design
— Successful teacher and program administrator
— Lay leader/member of various civic, community and service organizations
— Licensed real estate salesperson

EXPERIENCE:
1957–Present:	Free-lance crafts instructor
1986–Present:	Reading tutor for foreign-born children
1957–Present:	Free-lance dress tailor and designer of custom-made garments for children and women
1950–1977:	Family management
1968:	Staff advisor: Folk Arts Festival, Girl Scouts of the USA
1965–1968:	District Commissioner, Girl Scout Council of greater New York
1963–1965:	Assistant District Commissioner, Girl Scout Council of greater New York
1962–1965:	Program Director, Girl Scout Council of greater New York Queens Day Camp
1957–1963:	Troop leader, Girl Scout Council of greater New York
1944–1945:	Draper and assistant designer, Adrian's of Hollywood, Hollywood, California

EDUCATION:
1987:	Small business management course—Certificate New School for Social Research
1987:	Real estate sales licensing course—License
1970–1972:	Fashion Institute of Technology 15 credits completed toward A.A.S. degree
1941–1944:	Textile Trades High School—Diploma

REFERENCES FURNISHED UPON REQUEST

Sample Resume
Worker Moving into Management

Claire Simmonds
123 Montgomery Avenue
Pittsburgh, PA 15218
(912) 555-7772

OBJECTIVE   Position as Administrative Assistant

EXPERIENCE

January, 1986–
August, 1990

Lay Administrator
St. Benedict the Moor Church, Pittsburgh, PA

Entered computerized school records; updated approximately 150 financial records weekly; organized and managed recreational program for 350 students weekly; ordered supplies; scheduled volunteers; handled money. Also responsible for monthly accounting, filing, and budgeting.

October, 1972-
January, 1986

Assistant Sales Service Director
KDYV-TV, Pittsburgh, PA

Duties included: preparing a daily computerized commercial log, booking orders, filing, working with salespeople mainly via telephone to set up replacement spots.

Prior to 1972

Deposit Accounting Clerk
Union Bank, Pittsburgh, PA
Filed checks, verified signatures, rendered monthly statements.

VOLUNTEER EXPERIENCE

Chair, St. Benedict the Moor School Board
Board Member, Heights District Federal Credit Union
Board Member, Diocesan School Board

EDUCATION

St. John the Baptist High School
Diploma

REFERENCES   Available upon request

Resumes for Spanish Speakers

Muchas veces las personas olvidan que tienen aptitudes las cuales pueden ayudarlos a conseguir empleos de mejor pago aunque no hayan sido entrenados para un oficio específico. Comúnmente, estas aptitudes pueden ser relacionadas a un empleo.

Algunas de estas habilidades son:

1. Conocimiento de idiomas además del inglés.
2. Una licencia de manejar válida.
3. Poder llevarse bien con otras personas.
4. Tener la experiencia de haber trabajado en grupo con niños y adultos.
5. Poder supervisar otras personas (niños o adultos).
6. Pasatiempos o aficiones.
7. Haber viajado.
8. Haber leído libros o revistas sobre los tipos de trabajos o oficios en los que usted quiere trabajar.

Los resúmenes siguientes fueron escritos para personas que tienen algun tipo de experiencia laboral, pero poco entrenamiento. Vea como incluyen aptitudes y requisitos que no se desempeñaron en el trabajo mismo.

Si usted no tiene las habilidades necesarias para trabajar en un empleo técnico, de oficio o profesional, todavía puede escribir un resumen que cause una buena impresión a un patron debido a que usted está conciente de sus aptitudes y talentos, lo cual también es importante.

Guia Para un Resumen Simple en Orden Cronológico

Nombre

Dirección, ciudad, estado, código postal   Teléfono

Objetivo Profesional
(u Objetivo de Carrera, u Objetivo de Empleo)
Ejemplo: Busco posición como _____ que utilice mis habilidades.
Ejemplo: Busco posición de _____ que utilice mis antecedentes y experiencia en _____ y que utilice mis extensos conocimientos de _____.

**Diga en breve el tipo de posición que busca por cuanto ésta se relacione con su educación, su experiencia, y sus intereses.

Experiencia Particular
Título, Nombre de Compañía, localidad y fechas de cada empleo que tuvo (comience con el empleo más reciente)
***Use frases brevas y activas para describir las tareas y obligaciones
***Prepare una lista de sus logros y contribuciones
***Ud. puede incluir sus contribuciones voluntarias
***Use descripciones separadas para cada posición desempeñada dentro de la misma compañía, incluyendo fechas y promociones. Ejemplo: Obtuve promoción al departamento _____.

Otra Experiencia
Sección opcional en que se incluyen empleos anteriores o trabajo no relacionado. Use descripciones muy breves. Más vale no incluir esta experiencia si el título de la classificación es evidente por si mismo.

Educación
Título académico, especialización de curso, si ésta está relacionada con el empleo, institución académica (escuela secundaria, colegio o universidad), año de graduación, promedio de calificación si superior a 3.0. Incluya su educación si ha tomado cursos de adulto, su adiestramiento de trabajo, seminarios y conferencias, clases vocacionales, y cursos especializados si se relacionan con el empleo.

Organizaciones (o asociaciones, afiliaciones, actividades profesionales extracurriculares. Indique si era socio de algun club o asociación.)

Becas, Premios y Honores
Incluya becas, sociedades honorarias, premios honoríficos

Servicio Militar
Incluya el grado militar, entrenamiento especial y la fecha

Hechos Personales
Sección opcional para información tal como el hecho de que podría establecerse en un nuevo lugar, el deseo de hacer viajes, participación en las actividades de la comunidad, dominio de una lengua extranjera (también se puede incluir en la sección de Educación), intereses que se relacionan con el empleo, habilidades, las actividades en que le gusta participar durante su tiempo libre.

Muestra de Resumen
El Trabajador con Habilidades Poco Elevadas

Leon Jackson
345 Wescott Place
Cincinnati, Ohio 44534

Objetivo: Obtener una posición como empleado de surtido en una amplia organización
                 de venta al por menor.

Habilidades: Administrar el movimiento de grandes volúmenes de mercancía.
                 Supervisar el inventorio y preparar reportes inventariales.
                 Operar maquinarias de almacenes y equipo empaquetador.
                 Preciso con cifras.
                 Formal y confiable.
                 Habilidad para aprender rapidamente.
                 Capaz de asumir neuvas responsabilidades.
                 Bien organizado y eficiente.
                 Bilingüe en español e inglés.

Historial de Empleo:
1984–Al Presente: Empleado de Mercancía, ACME Supermarkets,
                     Almacén Principal.
                     Livingston, Ohio
1981–1983:   Empleado de Surtidos, Laurel Drug Store.
                     Repartidor, Laurel Drug Store.
Educación:
1987:   Diploma de equivalencia secundaria.
1983–1985:   Cincinnati Central Vocational High School.
                     Cursos en mantenimiento de edificios y reparación.

Muestra de Resumen
El Trabajador de Edad

Mary L. Henderson
798 East Haven Road
West Hartford, Connecticut 06041
203-555-0921

OBJETIVO: Administradora de Oficina o Secretaria Ejecutiva.

Experiencia Laboral:
1983–Al Presente Administradora de Oficina—Jones and Matthews, Dentist, Inc. Obligaciones: llevar los horarios, teneduría de libros órdenes de provisiones, cobro de cuentas, recepcionista y programadora de funciones.

1978–1983   Recepcionista—Daily, Hoyt, Parsons and Johnson, Attorneys. Obligaciones: operadora de cuadro de mandos, mecanografía y contacto con clientes.

Antes de 1978   Recepcionista—Mecanografía—Simmons Temporary Agency. Trabajo a medio tiempo con posiciones temporarias durante un período en el que obligaciones familiares no me permitieron mantener una posición de tiempo completo.

Habilidades: Conocimiento de procedimientos oficinales y equipos mecanografía: 90 palabras por minuto. Procesamiento de palabras y uso de programas y sistemas de programación PC como Multimate y Lotus 1-2-3.

                  Familiaridad con microcomputadores: IBM-PC y Apple IIe

Educación: Hartford Business College. Secretarial Course. West Hartford Schools. Un curso de educación adulta en procesamiento de palabras y aplicaciones de computadoras.

Servicios   West Hartford Schools: Secretaria PTA, Comité de levantamiento de fondos,
  Voluntarios: ayudante en la clase de mis hijos. Easter Cub Scouts: Madrina de cubil.

Las referencias están disponibles bajo petición.

PART III

Cover Letters
and References

Cover letters are very important. They are used to introduce yourself to prospective employers and to tell them why you are sending them your resume.

The Cover Letter

Keep the following eight points in mind when writing your cover letters:

1. Address your cover letter to a specific person. This should be the person most likely to hire you. You can call the company where you wish to work and ask for the person's name.

2. Make sure you tell the employer exactly what job you are applying for and, if it was announced in the want ads or some other place, how you heard about it.

3. Let the employer see that you know something about the company (what they do and how you can contribute).

4. Be enthusiastic in your letter without overdoing it.

5. Tell the employer about one unique quality you have and how it relates to the job you want. This could be in addition to what appears on your resume.

6. Be brief and businesslike. Make sure your typed cover letter is picture perfect with no errors.

7. Let the employer know that you will contact them within several days. (A week after you send your letter and resume is usually a good amount of time.)

8. Do not send photocopies or carbon copies of your cover letters. You must send an original letter to each employer. The letter should be typed on the same kind of paper as the resume.

Here are the two sample cover letters. The first example accompanies a resume sent in response to an advertised job opening. The second example is an "inquiry-query" letter accompanying a resume and sent to inquire about possible openings.

Sample Cover Letter
Response to an Advertised Job Opening

901 East Main Street
Flourville, PA 19701

November 25, 1991

Allied Home Services
Attn: Ms. Cynthia Jones
742 Graham Avenue
Philadelphia, PA 19104

Dear Ms. Jones:

I wish to be considered for the position of Team Leader as advertised in the Daily Record of November 24. My varied experience, language skills (English, French, Spanish), and my ability to work well with and supervise others would be of great benefit to a company such as yours.

I look forward to meeting you and will call next Monday to arrange an interview. Thank you for your consideration.

Very truly yours,

Maria Delas

Maria Delas

Sample Cover Letter
Inquiry about Possible Openings

1205 Orange Road
Nassau, NY 11736
November 10, 1991

Jones-Carlton Chevrolet
Mr. Richard Carlton
Vice President
1002 Fifth Street
Miller Place, NY 11511

Dear Mr. Carlton:

I am a self-employed auto mechanic and am now looking for a job with a large and busy dealership such as yours. My skills and knowledge include foreign and domestic cars, trucks, and vans, and I have recently become a registered auto mechanic in the state of New York. I know that your customers would always receive quality, efficient service from me, and I am eager to learn more about the automotive business from you and your staff.

I will call you in a few days to schedule an appointment to talk more about my working with Jones-Carlton.

Very truly yours,

George West

George West

The Marketing Letter

The marketing letter, also known as the resume letter, is more like a long cover letter than a resume and is often used in place of both. Details are condensed and presented in a single letter format. Dates and names of employers are rarely mentioned. The single advantage of a marketing letter over a cover letter and resume is adaptability to specific positions. It gives you a greater degree of flexibility in presenting all your strengths and accomplishments that are relevant to the job you are after.

Generally the marketing letter is sent to prospective employers or to individuals who might provide useful job search information and referrals. It may also be used in response to an ad requesting resumes. Here are some pointers for writing marketing letters:

- In the marketing letter you may choose the information you wish to include or omit from your background.

- A cover letter usually describes one or two accomplishments. A marketing letter may include as many as ten or more.

- With few exceptions, marketing letters should be typed on high-quality white bond paper and sent in white business envelopes.

- A marketing letter should open with a strong statement to hook the reader. Paragraphs should be short and to the point. Emphasis should be on skills rather than on training.

Sample
Marketing Letter

2012 Front St.
Berea, OH 44142

Mrs. Sarah Smith
491 Charles St.
Cleveland, OH 44112

Dear Ms. Smith,

A notice of your new store that will open shortly at the Shore Shopping Center caught my attention. An appliance store specializing in ranges and microwaves will be a welcome addition in this part of the city. My interest is both as a customer and as a potential employee. I have targeted appliance demonstration and sales as my primary occupational objective.

There are many reasons why I am qualified for such work:

- Seven years experience in appliance demonstration/sales.
- Extensive personal experience (five years) with a microwave oven.
- Experience teaching microwave cooking classes.
- Supervisory experience.

My work experience was with the East End Power Company and involved demonstrating new stoves to individual consumers and managers of retail outlets. This experience provided me the opportunity to develop techniques that subsequently improved sales 10% in a one-year period. The company honored me for this achievement.

Microwave cooking has become an important method of meal preparation. I have become adept at using mine both for my family and in preparing classes for our local Adult Education Center. One of the things I've done is prepare my own cookbook for students. I'm enclosing my favorite chicken recipe.

The Home Economics in Business Association sponsors continuing education seminars. I have taken advantage of several of these relating to management and current business practices.

My unique background and personal experience would be useful additions to your sales force. I'll call this week in hopes that we can arrange a meeting to discuss any possibilities with your firm.

Sincerely,

Mary Field

enclosure

Sample
Marketing Letter

524 Avery Lane
Tulsa, Oklahoma 59304
402-555-1234

October 3, 1991

Mrs. S. Jones
Personnel Director
ABC Inc.
2920 N. Cleveland St.
Tulsa, OK 52124

Dear Mrs. Jones:

I am writing in response to your ad for an office clerk in the Tulsa Times on September 28. I have heard and read many favorable things about your company, and I feel that this would be the perfect work environment. The fact that ABC Inc. is a small but rapidly expanding company presents some interesting challenges, and I am very interested in the available position.

Your ad stated that ABC Inc. is looking for someone with experience in general office skills. I have been involved in this line of work for many years. Through volunteer and paid positions, I have learned the skills of typing, budgeting, filing, answering telephones and correspondence, greeting customers, and running standard office equipment.

Specifically, I have had considerable experience typing business correspondence. My typing speed is 65 wpm. I have also put together many statistical and financial reports and am familiar with many different types of forms including inventory and tax forms. I have also been responsible for typing activity bulletins and putting together a newsletter for the local PTA. I also have had direct involvement with maintaining filing systems for several organizations. In one instance, I maintained a system for a firm with over 300 clients.

I have also had experience with customer relations, including answering telephones. In several of my job experiences, I was responsible for greeting clients and answering questions the public may have. Routing mail and delivering messages has been part of my training.

I have hands-on experience with all major office equipment including word processors and photocopiers. I have also become familiar with desktop publishing systems through my experience with the PTA newsletter.

I have spent the majority of my life in this field, as well as having taken secretarial training courses at Tulsa Community College. I know the business world well, and what I don't know I'm willing and eager to learn. I need very little job instruction—I am capable of taking a project and completing it on my own. I have also worked on many team projects and have found that just as rewarding. I work well with other people and can be counted on to pull my share of the weight.

My work experience has also taught me how to work under pressure. I have often had to work under pressing deadlines and am willing to work longer hours or whatever it takes to meet a deadline.

For a growing company such as ABC Inc., efficiency is very important. I believe that I could be a contribution to ABC Inc. by increasing efficiency in the office. I will call you at the end of the week to schedule a convenient time to discuss more about my working for ABC Inc. Thank you for your consideration.

Sincerely,

Alice Jensen

Alice Jensen

References

Often a job listing asks for one or more letters of recommendation, or for references. The following suggestions will help you request a reference from anyone:

1. Choose a person who knows your abilities. Ask people ahead of time if you may use them as references or if they will write a letter of recommendation.

2. If possible, make an appointment to ask the person to write the letter of recommendation. Allow 10 to 14 days for the completion of the letter.

3. If it is not possible to meet with the persons, telephone to ask permission to use them as references, and follow up with a letter.

4. Give the person a stamped envelope addressed to the employer, a copy of the job listing, a statement about your strengths and skills, and a copy of your resume.

5. Write a short thank-you note to each person who helped you.

Bibliography of Books on Resume Writing

Action—Getting Resumes for Today's Jobs
Turbak, Gary   Arco   1983
How to build a resume and choose the right language for the job.

Better Resumes for Computer Personnel
Lewis, Adele   Barron's   1984
Sample resumes for computer-related positions at all levels.

Better Resumes for Executives and Professionals
Wilson, Robert   Barron's   1983
Resumes aimed at jobs dealing with eight standard corporate functions such as communications, finance, marketing, etc. Includes those focusing on changing careers.

Better Resumes for Sales and Marketing Personnel
Lewis, Adele   Barron's   1985
Covers retail and wholesale sales, regional sales managers, market research, entry-level through executive jobs.

The Damn Good Resume Guide
Parker, Yana   Ten Speed Press   1983
How to focus on your strong points through a job objective, skills assessment, work history, and education and training.

Developing a Professional Vita or Resume
McDaniels, Carl   Virginia Polytechnic Institute   1978
How to present professional qualifications and activities in the most meaningful way.

Does Your Resume Wear Blue Jeans?
Good, Edward C.   The Word Store   1985
A folksy approach for college and high school students.

How to Write a Winning Resume
Bloch, Deborah Perlmutter   VGM Career Horizons   1989
A step-by-step approach to writing your resume. Includes numerous worksheets and sample resumes.

How to Write Better Resumes
Lewis, Adele   Barron's   1983
Details five basic resume styles with 120 models covering nearly 300 job categories, from recent graduate to executive.

Liberal Arts Power: How to Sell It on Your Resume
Nadler, Burton   Peterson's   1985
How to create a targeted resume by matching a liberal arts background to specific job requirements.

The Perfect Resume
Jackson, Tom   Anchor Books   1990
One of the best guides to producing a resume that will express skills and qualifications clearly and effectively. Uses the Career Discovery Process to assist readers in discovery and definition of their career goals and job targets.

The Professional Resume and Job Search Guide

Dickhut, Harold W.   Prentice-Hall   1981

Step-by-step guide for organizing material to show areas of knowledge and areas of achievement with a wide range of sample resumes and special guidelines for student resumes.

Resume and Job Hunting Guide for Present and Future Veterans

DePrez, Caroline   Arco   1984

All the details for collecting and selecting data and building the resume.

The Resume Handbook: How to Write Outstanding Resumes and Cover Letters for Every Situation

Hizer, David V.   Bob Adams   1985

Good sections on cover letters and marketing letters; examples of best and worst resumes.

The Resume Kit

Beatty, Richard   John Wiley and Sons   1984

The resume as seen through the eyes of the employment manager, identifying quick "knock-out" factors which eliminate the job seeker.

Resumes for College Graduates

Lewis, William   Monarch Press   1984

Specially designed for college graduates without much work experience, to help them find their first job.

Resumes for Communications Careers

Editors of VGM   VGM Career Horizons   1991

Dozens of sample resumes and cover letters for people seeking employment in the many different fields of communications.

Resumes for Computer Professionals

Shanahan, William F.   Arco   1983

Analysis of 40 sample resumes showing how features can be combined to emphasize computer-related skills at all levels of expertise.

Resumes for Engineers

Shanahan, William F.   Arco   1983

Forty-one resumes have been designed to meet the needs of recent engineering graduates as well as professional with varying years of experience.

Resumes for Executives and Professionals

Shykind, Maury   Arco   1984

Self-marketing strategy for many managerial positions.

Resumes for Sales and Marketing

Faux, Marian   Monarch   1982

Chronological and achievement-oriented resumes are designed to sell the job applicant.

Resumes for Sales and Marketing Careers
Editors of VGM   VGM Career Horizons   1991

Information and pointers on writing an effective resume, followed by 100 pages of sample resumes and 20 pages of sample cover letters.

Resumes for Secretaries
Corwen, Leonard   Arco   1985

Sample resumes dealing with specialized skills for a variety of secretarial positions.

Resumes for Paralegals and Other People with Legal Training
Berkey, Rachel   Arco   1983

Forty sample resumes for paralegals, legal secretaries, court personnel, and other law-related jobs.

Resumes for Technicians
Shanahan, William F.   Arco   1983

Covers areas of surveying, engineering, drafting, construction, and electronics.

Resumes That Work
Cowan, Tom   NAL   1983

How to write three basic types of resumes. Sample resumes by field. Good examples of cover letters.

Resumes: The Nitty Gritty
Kennedy, Joyce Lain   Sun Features   1989

Syndicated columnist on careers developed a guide to better resume writing.

Resumes: The Write Stuff
Miller, Robin   Garrett Park Press   1987

Before and after—how to make over your resume.

Revising Your Resume
Schruman, Nancy   John Wiley & Sons   1986

Sixty rules for success, with samples illustrating each rule.

Writing a Job Winning Resume   Prentice-Hall   1980
A step-by-step guide that has a section for people with special problems.

In addition, most books covering techniques of job hunting include chapters on resume writing. Those written for special audiences often deal with considerations unique to their readers. Examples are *Career Changing,* by Linda Kline, and *Connecting: A Handbook for Housewives Returning to Paid Work,* by Sally Ashley.

Skill Groupings
 List

The following is a listing of skills that are commonly called for when working in the occupational fields that appear in boldface type. Use these words and descriptions on your resume to help communicate your skills and assets.

Administration
See **Management**

Analysis
Evaluating
Examining
Drafting

Architectural Design
Analyzing proposed
functions
Assessing existing
facilities
Building models
Executing working
drawings
Planning lighting and
furniture layout
Planning office layout
Planning space

Arts
Acting
Announcing
Arranging
Carving
Composing
Creating
Dancing
Decorating
Demonstrating
Designing
Directing
Dramatizing
Drawing
Expressing
Forming
Lettering
Memorizing
Miming
Painting
Performing
Photographing
Playing
Retouching
Sewing
Singing
Shaping

Aviation
Checking
Commanding
Flying
Operating

Bookkeeping
Billing monthly fees and
expenses to 30 client
divisions
Monthly bank
reconciliations
Posting to accounts
receivable and payable
and cash receipts
Preparing monthly
financial statements
and semimonthly
payroll

Buying (Retail)
Exceeding holiday sales
plan for both
departments by 15%
Organization and
execution of
merchandising plans

Communications
Acting
Advocating
Assisting
Convincing
Counseling
Demonstrating
Editing
Explaining
Expressing
Influencing
Interpreting
Interviewing
Listening
Negotiating
Persuading
Presenting
Reporting
Suggesting
Translating
Writing

Community Relations
Conducting tours
Group facilitating
Public relations
Public speaking
Rapport development
Presenting information
and referral services to
social, professional, and
educational groups

Comparing
Arranging
Selecting
Sorting

Compiling
Classifying
Collating
Gathering

Computer Programming
Analyzing flowcharts
Creating structured
programs
Debugging programs
Establishing a coded
language

Construction
Building
Installing
Operating
Plastering

Coordination
Adapting
Administering
Appraising
Auditing
Budgeting
Computing
Distributing
Evaluating
Examining
Executing
Expanding
Guiding
Improving
Inspecting
Liaison
Overseeing
Reporting

Reviewing
Scheduling
Strengthening
Coordinating manpower
training program
Financial analysis
Getting cooperation
Group coordination
Procedure development
Quality assessment
System development

Copying
Transcribing

Cost Control
Improving profit of truck
fleet by 34% but
keeping operating costs
below common carrier
rates

Counseling
Career direction
Coaching and
encouraging clients to
develop self-confidence
and to make the most of
their skills and
qualities
Developing interviewing
skills
Meeting with clients in
ongoing counseling
relationships
Outplacement
Teaching job search and
resume writing

Directing
See **Management**

Education
Analyzing
Converting
Designing
Measuring
Preparing
Surveying

Finance
Accounting
Advising
Analyzing
Auditing
Computing

Designing
Estimating
Examining
Forecasting
Interpreting
Judging
Planning
Preparing
Solving
Studying

Food Service
Catering
Cooling
Cutting
Peeling
Preparing
Serving
Washing

Hairstyling
Bleaching
Curling
Cutting
Dyeing
Shampooing
Shaping
Shaving
Tinting

Health
Analyzing
Diagnosing
Examining
Measuring
Preventing
Providing
Specializing
Testing
Treating
Familiar with medical
  terminology

**Heavy Equipment
  Operator**
Driving
Operating
Tending

Hospitality
Attending
Directing
Guiding

Planning
Providing
Serving
Welcoming

Human Relations
Advocating
Assisting
Communicating
Convincing
Counseling
Demonstrating
Explaining
Helping
Influencing
Interpreting
Interviewing
Listening
Negotiating
Persuading
Presenting
Reporting
Suggesting
Teaching
Training

Instruction
See **Teaching**

Law Enforcement
Analyzing
Arresting
Collecting
Commanding
Enforcing
Examining
Guarding
Inspecting
Investigating
Patrolling
Policy making
Preventing
Questioning
Regulating

**Management and
  Supervision**
Advising
Analyzing
Approving
Arranging
Assigning

Bargaining
Coaching
Computing
Conducting
Contacting
Contracting
Delegating
Developing
Directing
Encouraging
Explaining
Hiring
Identifying
Imitating
Implementing
Innovating
Instructing
Managing

Meeting
Motivating
Negotiating
Operating
Organizing
Overseeing
Persuading
Planning
Preparing
Presiding
Purchasing
Running
Serving
Solving
Submitting
Supervising
Writing

- Coordinating reorganization of total service delivery system, including work assignments, resource updating, classification and data collection

- Coordinating setup of new garment rental customers

- Developing personnel policies and procedures manual

- Evaluating performance

- Interpreting and communicating company policy

- Managing and directing employment service operation and unemployment compensation program

- Motivating employees

- Overseeing agency expenditures

- Planning budget proposals

- Planning, directing, coordinating job placement services

- Preparing monthly payrolls

- Preparing and interpreting monthly financial statement

- Recording all financial transactions

- Solving problems

- Supervising, training, and scheduling employees

- Supervising 20 employees

- Training new and temporary route-salespeople

Marketing
  Researching need and use
    of new products

Materials Control
  Collecting

Counting
Issuing
Packing
Placing
Recording
Shipping
Unpacking
Weighing

Mechanical
Adjusting
Building
Greasing
Maintenance
Making
Operating
Replacing
Tuning

Mechanics
Adjusting
Altering
Guiding
Placing
Repairing
Replacing
Restoring
Setting up

Modeling
Posing

Museum
Leading tours of schools
  and college classes
Preparing exhibitions
Preparing/delivering
  lectures and gallery
  talks

Office Work
Analyzing

Billing
Bookkeeping
Checking
Classifying
Collecting
Compiling
Computing
Dispatching
Entering
Filing
Gathering
Inspecting
Interviewing
Mailing
Maintaining
Operating
Organizing
Preparing
Receiving
Recording
Record keeping
Registering
Reviewing
Routing
Scheduling
Sending
Sorting
Transcribing
Typing
Verifying
Wrapping

- Answering telephone calls and taking messages
- Composing correspondence
- Greeting clients
- Making international telephone calls
- Operating a cash register
- Taking shorthand
- Typing correspondence, accounting, reports, manuscripts and theses
- Typing legal documents
- Typing 70 w.p.m.

Operation
Adjusting
Checking
Controlling
Monitoring
Setting up

Starting
Stopping

Organization
Administering
Analyzing

Arranging	Diagnosing
Assigning	Editing
Beautifying	Imaging
Cataloging	Innovating
Collecting	Inventing
Creating	Recruiting
Designing	Researching
Detailing	Reviewing
Developing	Surveying

- Designing programs to suit groups differing in size and makeup
- Follow through, hiring, training, supervising, scheduling
- Initiating/developing program proposal—securing funds
- Managing
- Organizing job-seeking class
- Organizing meetings, tours, speakers, and travel arrangements
- Overseeing $300,000 budget, staffing, community program and outreach
- Planning and coordination
- Policy development
- Problem solving
- Program design
- Project design
- Setting priorities
- Team building
- Training design
- Troubleshooting

Outdoors
Exercising
Farming
Feeding
Fishing
Grooming
Harvesting
Logging
Mixing
Planting
Raising
Selecting
Sharpening
Spraying
Studying
Tending
Training

People Skills
Coaching
Consulting
Diverting
Entertaining
Helping
Instructing
Mentoring
Negotiating
Persuading
Serving
Speaking
Supervising

Persuading
Influencing

Personnel

- Administering sexual harassment guidelines
- Assisting in development of competency based criteria for performance evaluation
- Completing employee evaluations for salary increases
- Conducting orientation programs
- Conducting safety meetings with drivers
- Coordinating Affirmative Action plan and reporting
- Developing policies and procedures manual
- Handling all personnel injury and property damage claims
- Handling OSHA and EEOC requirements for 17 U.S. facilities
- Hiring drivers, warehouse workers and office personnel
- Improving working relations with salaried and hourly workers, resulting in improved productivity and attitudes
- Interviewing and hiring
- Interviewing and placing employees
- Investigating and resolving personnel complaints with three unions
- Knowledgeable about EEO and Affirmative Action
- Planning and conducting miniworkshops on proposal writing
- Recruiting, interviewing, prescreening, testing, job development and placement
- Rewriting employee handbook

Placement

- Contacting employees and training representatives
- Cooperating with other agencies in presenting joint programs
- Placing clients in appropriate employment or training situations

Planning

Administering	Detailing
Analyzing	Developing
Arranging	Diagnosing
Assigning	Editing
Beautifying	Imagining
Cataloging	Innovating
Collecting	Inventing
Creating	Recruiting
Communicating	Researching
Controlling	Reviewing
Designing	Surveying

- Follow through
- Initiating/developing program proposal; securing funding
- Planning, implementing, evaluating 233k-long personal growth and group process experience
- Planning, implementing, evaluating educational experiences on decision-making skills, planning and goal setting skills, leadership skills, listening and communication skills
- Planning, organizing, supervising, informational seminars
- Planning training meetings for 20–200 people
- Policy development
- Problem solving
- Program design
- Project design
- Setting priorities
- Team building
- Training design
- Trouble shooting

Police
See **Law Enforcement**

Problem Solving
  Reviewing and evaluating
    systems and reports

**Production
    (Manufacturing)**
  Cutting
  Loading
  Operating
  Polishing
  Setting up
  Sewing
  Sorting
  Stapling
  Tending

Unloading
Welding

Public Relations
  Advertising
  Contacting
  Creating
  Designing
  Directing
  Graphics
  Influencing
  Layout
  Preparing
  Promoting
  Raising funds
  Speaking
  Writing

- Coordinating all news releases internally and to the media
- Creating and producing audiovisual presentations
- Developing and producing promotional literature
- Initiating and maintaining year-round public relations programs through the news media, industry, labor, schools, churches and speaking engagements
  Preparing/delivering lectures and gallery talks
  Preparing exhibitions

Quality Control
Checking
Control
Estimating
Examining
Grading
Inspecting

Religious
Advising
Assisting
Comforting
Counseling
Helping
Preaching

Real Estate Sales

- 90% of listings resulted in sales
- Provided technical information on construction
- Sold homes with total value of 3.5 million dollars
- Successfully negotiated 85% of purchase offers

Sales

Advising
Assisting
Computing
Demonstrating
Driving
Explaining
Helping

Influencing
Persuading
Providing
Purchasing
Quoting
Selecting
Talking

- Closing major accounts
- Contacting architects, managers, owners and purchasing agents
- Covering established and new accounts
- Doubling business in one existing account
- Establishing long-term working relationships with customers by emphasizing service
- Expediting purchase orders and contract orders
- Initiating major new accounts
- Organizing territories and promotions
- Preparing proposals
- Promoting and selling
- Supervising subcontractor installation

Sales (Route)
- Delivering and selling
- Responsible for safe, timely delivery, taking customer's orders, filling orders
- Setting up lockers and displays

Science
Analyzing
Conducting
Developing
Evaluating
Examining
Experimenting
Explaining

Mounting
Recording
Researching
Solving
Staining
Studying
Testing

Service
Assigning
Attending
Carrying
Delivering
Handing out
Mixing
Operating
Ushering
Waiting on

Social Research
Analyzing
Describing
Interpreting
Reporting
Writing

Social Services
Assisting
Counseling
Guiding
Helping
Investigating
Placing

Sports
Balancing
Coaching
Competing
Demonstrating
Judging
Juggling
Inspecting
Penalizing
Playing
Practicing
Riding
Stopping
Swimming
Timing

Supervision
See **Management**

Teaching
Conducting
Demonstrating
Explaining
Instructing
Planning
Producing
Training

Things (Working with)
Adjusting
Controlling
Lifting
Pulling
Pushing

Training and Development
- Designing and implementing program on effective organization development skills for hospital staff
- Designing instructional materials
- Modifying training content based on assessments and evaluations
- Supervising and conducting staff development workshops for 10 people
- Supervising, coordinating, developing staff training
- Training hospital program staff (154) in policies and procedures
- Writing training department procedure manual

Transportation
Collecting
Driving
Inspecting
Moving
Operating

Writing
Analyzing
Creating
Criticism
Developing
Editing
Expressing
Revising
Writing

APPENDIX C

Action Words

When writing your resume, you should try to use as many action words (verbs) as you can. Action words liven up your resume and make it more interesting and readable to employers. The following is an alphabetical listing of action words (each given in three different forms) that you may wish to use in your resume.

accelerate
  accelerated
  accelerating

accomplish
  accomplished
  accomplishing

account
  accounted
  accounting

achieve
  achieved
  achieving

act
  acted
  acting

adapt
  adapted
  adapting

adjust
  adjusted
  adjusting

administer
  administered
  administering

advertise
  advertised
  advertising

advise
  advised
  advising

advocate
  advocated
  advocating

alter
  altered
  altering

analyze
  analyzed
  analyzing

appraise
  appraised
  appraising

approve
  approved
  approving

arbitrate
  arbitrated
  arbitrating

arrange
  arranged
  arranging

assemble
  assembled
  assembling

assign
  assigned
  assigning

assist
  assisted
  assisting

audit
  audited
  auditing

beautify
  beautified
  beautifying

budget
  budgeted
  budgeting

build
  built
  building

buy
  bought
  buying

calculate
calculated
calculating

carve
carved
carving

catalog
cataloged
cataloging

chart
charted
charting

check
checked
checking

classify
classified
classifying

clean
cleaned
cleaning

coach
coached
coaching

collate
collated
collating

collect
collected
collecting

command
commanded
commanding

communicate
communicated
communicating

compare
compared
comparing

compute
computed
computing

complete
completed
completing

compose
composed
composing

compound
compounded
compounding

conceptualize
conceptualized
conceptualizing

conduct
conducted
conducting

confront
confronted
confronting

conserve
conserved
conserving

construct
constructed
constructing

consult
consulted
consulting

contact
contacted
contacting

contribute
contributed
contributing

control
controlled
controlling

convert
converted
converting

cook
cooked
cooking

cooperate
  cooperated
  cooperating

copy
  copied
  copying

coordinate
  coordinated
  coordinating

correspond
  corresponded
  corresponding

counsel
  counseled
  counseling

count
  counted
  counting

create
  created
  creating

critique
  critiqued
  critiquing

defend
  defended
  defending

delegate
  delegated
  delegating

deliver
  delivered
  delivering

demonstrate
  demonstrated
  demonstrating

design
  designed
  designing

detect
  detected
  detecting

determine
  determined
  determining

develop
  developed
  developing

devise
  devised
  devising

diagnose
  diagnosed
  diagnosing

direct
  directed
  directing

discover
  discovered
  discovering

dispense
  dispensed
  dispensing

display
  displayed
  displaying

distribute
  distributed
  distributing

divert
  diverted
  diverting

double
  doubled
  doubling

draft
  drafted
  drafting

dramatize
  dramatized
  dramatizing

draw
  drawn
  drawing

drive
  driven
  driving

edit
  edited
  editing

eliminate
  eliminated
  eliminating

encourage
  encouraged
  encouraging

enforce
  enforced
  enforcing

enter
  entered
  entering

entertain
  entertained
  entertaining

establish
  established
  establishing

estimate
  estimated
  estimating

evaluate
  evaluated
  evaluating

examine
  examined
  examining

exchange
  exchanged
  exchanging

execute
  executed
  executing

exercise
  exercised
  exercising

exhibit
  exhibited
  exhibiting

expand
  expanded
  expanding

experiment
  experimented
  experimenting

explain
  explained
  explaining

express
  expressed
  expressing

facilitate
  facilitated
  facilitating

feed
  fed
  feeding

file
  filed
  filing

find
  found
  finding

fix
  fixed
  fixing

follow
  followed
  following

forecast
  forecasted
  forecasting

formulate
  formulated
  formulating

gain
  gained
  gaining

gather
  gathered
  gathering

generate
  generated
  generating

give
  gave
  giving

guard
  guarded
  guarding

guide
  guided
  guiding

handle
  handled
  handling

harvest
  harvested
  harvesting

heal
  healed
  healing

help
  helped
  helping

increase
  increased
  increasing

identify
  identified
  identifying

influence
  influenced
  influencing

imagine
  imagined
  imagining

implement
  implemented
  implementing

improve
  improved
  improving

initiate
  initiated
  initiating

innovate
  innovated
  innovating

inspect
  inspected
  inspecting

inspire
  inspired
  inspiring

install
  installed
  installing

instruct
  instructed
  instructing

interpret
  interpreted
  interpreting

interview
  interviewed
  interviewing

introduce
  introduced
  introducing

invent
  invented
  inventing

investigate
  investigated
  investigating

judge
  judged
  judging

landscape
  landscaped
  landscaping

launch
  launched
  launching

lay
  laid
  laying

lead
  led
  leading

learn
  learned
  learning

lift
  lifted
  lifting

listen
  listened
  listening

loan
  loaned
  loaning

locate
  located
  locating

mail
  mailed
  mailing

maintain
  maintained
  maintaining

manage
  managed
  managing

message
  messaged
  messaging

measure
  measured
  measuring

mediate
  mediated
  mediating

meet
  met
  meeting

mentor
  mentored
  mentoring

merchandise
  merchandised
  merchandising

model
  modeled
  modeling

modify
  modified
  modifying

monitor
  monitored
  monitoring

memorize
  memorized
  memorizing

motivate
  motivated
  motivating

move
  moved
  moving

negotiate
  negotiated
  negotiating

obtain
  obtained
  obtaining

operate
  operated
  operating

order
  ordered
  ordering

organize
  organized
  organizing

package
  packaged
  packaging

pack
  packed
  packing

paint
  painted
  painting

patrol
  patrolled
  patrolling

perform
  performed
  performing

persuade
  persuaded
  persuading

plan
  planned
  planning

plant
  planted
  planting

plaster
  plastered
  plastering

play
  played
  playing

polish
  polished
  polishing

pose
  posed
  posing

post
  posted
  posting

preach
  preached
  preaching

prepare
  prepared
  preparing

prescribe
  prescribed
  prescribing

present
  presented
  presenting

preside
  presided
  presiding

prevent
  prevented
  preventing

print
  printed
  printing

process
  processed
  processing

produce
  produced
  producing

program
  programmed
  programming

project
  projected
  projecting

promote
  promoted
  promoting

propose
  proposed
  proposing

protect
  protected
  protecting

provide
  provided
  providing

pump
  pumped
  pumping

purchase
  purchased
  purchasing

question
  questioned
  questioning

quote
  quoted
  quoting

raise
  raised
  raising

read
  read
  reading

realize
  realized
  realizing

receive
  received
  receiving

recognize
  recognized
  recognizing

recommend
  recommended
  recommending

record
  recorded
  recording

recruit
  recruited
  recruiting

redesign
  redesigned
  redesigning

reduce
  reduced
  reducing

refer
  referred
  referring

register
  registered
  registering

rehabilitate
  rehabilitated
  rehabilitating

relieve
  relieved
  relieving

remember
  remembered
  remembering

remove
  removed
  removing

render
  rendered
  rendering

reorganize
  reorganized
  reorganizing

repair
  repaired
  repairing

repeat
  repeated
  repeating

replace
  replaced
  replacing

report
  reported
  reporting

represent
  represented
  representing

research
  researched
  researching

restore
  restored
  restoring

review
  reviewed
  reviewing

revise
  revised
  revising

revitalize
  revitalized
  revitalizing

ride
  rode
  riding

route
  routed
  routing

run
  ran
  running

save
  saved
  saving

schedule
  scheduled
  scheduling

sculpt
  sculpted
  sculpting

seat
  seated
  seating

select
  selected
  selecting

sell
  sold
  selling

send
  sent
  sending

service
  serviced
  servicing

serve
  served
  serving

sew
  sewed
  sewing

shampoo
  shampooed
  shampooing

shape
  shaped
  shaping

shave
  shaved
  shaving

simplify
  simplified
  simplifying

sing
  sang
  singing

sketch
  sketched
  sketching

solve
  solved
  solving

sort
  sorted
  sorting

speak
  spoke
  speaking

start
  started
  starting

streamline
  streamlined
  streamlining

strengthen
  strengthened
  strengthening

stress
  stressed
  stressing

stretch
  stretched
  stretching

structure
  structured
  structuring

study
  studied
  studying

style
  styled
  styling

succeed
  succeeded
  succeeding

suggest
  suggested
  suggesting

summarize
  summarized
  summarizing

supercede
  superceded
  superceding

supervise
  supervised
  supervising

supply
  supplied
  supplying

support
  supported
  supporting

survey
  surveyed
  surveying

swim
  swam
  swimming

synthesize
  synthesized
  synthesizing

tailor
  tailored
  tailoring

talk
  talked
  talking

teach
  taught
  teaching

tend
  tended
  tending

terminate
  terminated
  terminating

test
  tested
  testing

time
  timed
  timing

tint
  tinted
  tinting

tolerate
  tolerated
  tolerating

trace
  traced
  tracing

track
  tracked
  tracking

trade
  traded
  trading

train
  trained
  training

transfer
  transferred
  transferring

transcribe
  transcribed
  transcribing

treat
  treated
  treating

trim
  trimmed
  trimming

triple
  tripled
  tripling

tune
  tuned
  tuning

turn
  turned
  turning

tutor
  tutored
  tutoring

type
  typed
  typing

usher
  ushered
  ushering

verify
  verified
  verifying

visualize
  visualized
  visualizing

wash
  washed
  washing

weigh
  weighed
  weighing

welcome
  welcomed
  welcoming

widen
  widened
  widening

win
  won
  winning

wrap
  wrapped
  wrapping